anythink

D1122957

Black Bear

Published in the United States of America by Cherry Lake Publishing
Ann Arbor, Michigan
www.cherrylakepublishing.com

Reading Adviser: Marla Conn MS, Ed., Literacy specialist, Read-Ability, Inc.
Book Design: Jennifer Wahi
Illustrator: Jeff Bane

Photo Credits: © NaturesMomentsuk / Shutterstock.com, 5; © critterbiz / Shutterstock.com, 7; © Josef Pittner / Shutterstock.com, 9; © jadimages / Shutterstock.com, 11; © dannybregman / Shutterstock.com, 13; © Troutnut / Shutterstock.com, 15; © Christopher MacDonald / Shutterstock.com, 17; © Don Mammoser / Shutterstock.com, 19; © Agustin Esmoris / Shutterstock.com, 21; © Dennis W Donohue / Shutterstock.com, 23; © Ozerina Anna 2-3, 24; Cover, 1, 6, 16, 18, 20, Jeff Bane

Library of Congress Cataloging-in-Publication Data has been filed and is available at catalog.loc.gov

Printed in the United States of America
Corporate Graphics

About the author: Dr. Virginia Loh-Hagan is an author, university professor, former classroom teacher, and curriculum designer. Her favorite bears are pandas and moon bears. She lives in San Diego with her very tall husband and very naughty dogs. To learn more about her, visit www.virginialoh.com.

About the illustrator: Jeff Bane and his two business partners own a studio along the American River in Folsom, California, home of the 1849 Gold Rush. When Jeff's not sketching or illustrating for clients, he's either swimming or kayaking in the river to relax.

Most black bears are black or brown. Spirit bears live in Canada. They are white black bears.

Black bears have sharp claws.
The claws are short and black.
They are **hooked**. The claws help
black bears climb. Claws help
them find food.

Males are bigger than females. Males weigh about 300 pounds (136 kilograms). Bears can be 3 feet (91 centimeters) tall when on all fours. They are 5 feet long (152 cm).

Black bears live in North America. They're the smallest bears in North America. They're the most common bears.

Black bears live in the woods. They live in mountains. They live by rivers and trees. They like to be able to hide.

Black bears eat grass and roots. They eat berries and bugs. They eat honey. They eat fish and even **mammals**.

Black bears have a long tongue that helps them find food. They find food alone. They hunt alone. Black bears are **solitary**.

Black bears can run fast and swim well. They see well. They hear well. They smell well.

What do you do in the spring?

Black bears eat a lot in summer and fall. They **store** up fat. Black bears **hibernate** in winter. They sleep in dens. They live on their body fat.

Sows are female bears. They have cubs. Cubs are born in dens. In the spring, sows and cubs leave the den. They look for food.

glossary

hibernate (HYE-bur-nate) to sleep in the winter

hooked (HUKD) shaped like a curve

mammals (MAM-uhlz) animals that have hair and give birth to live babies; their body temperature stays the same no matter where they live

solitary (SAH-lih-ter-ee) being alone

sows (SOUZ) female bears

store (STOR) to build up, to keep

index